Shih Tzu
and Other Toy Dogs

Editorial:
Editor in Chief: Paul A. Kobasa
Project Manager: Cassie Mayer
Senior Editor: Christine Sullivan
Writer: Marta Segal Block
Researcher: Cheryl Graham
Manager, Contracts & Compliance
  (Rights & Permissions): Loranne K. Shields
Indexer: David Pofelski

Graphics and Design:
Manager: Tom Evans
Coordinator, Design Development
  and Production: Brenda B. Tropinski
Photographs Editor: Kathy Creech
Cartographer: John Rejba

Pre-Press and Manufacturing:
Director: Carma Fazio
Manufacturing Manager:
  Steven K. Hueppchen
Production/Technology Manager:
  Anne Fritzinger

For information about other World Book publications, visit our Web site at http://www.worldbookonline.com or call 1-800-WORLDBK (967-5325).

For information about sales to schools and libraries, call 1-800-975-3250 (United States), or 1-800-837-5365 (Canada).

World Book, Inc.
233 N. Michigan Avenue
Chicago, IL 60601
U.S.A.

Library of Congress Cataloging-in-Publication Data
Shih tzu and other toy dogs.
    p. cm. -- (World Book's animals of the world)
  Includes index.
    Summary: "An introduction to Shih Tzu and other toy dogs, presented in a highly illustrated, question-and-answer format. Features include fun facts, glossary, resource list, index, and scientific classification list"-- Provided by publisher.
  ISBN 978-0-7166-1372-5
  1. Toy dogs--Juvenile literature. 2. Shih tzu--Juvenile literature. I. World Book, Inc.
  SF429.T7S55 2010
  636.76--dc22
                                        2009020169

World Book's Animals of the World
Set 6: ISBN: 978-0-7166-1365-7
Printed in China by Leo Paper Products LTD., Heshan, Guangdong
1st printing November 2009

Picture Acknowledgments: Cover: © Jason Lugo, istockphoto; © Petronilo G. Dangoy Jr., Shutterstock; © pixshots/Shutterstock; © WizData/Shutterstock; © Melvinlee, Dreamstime.

© tbkmedia/Alamy Images 39; AP Images 59; © Dreamstime 15, 25, 45, 47, 59; © AFP/Getty Images 9; © Yale Joel, Time Life Pictures/Getty Images 11; istockphoto 7, 17, 21, 55; © Gus Chan, The Plain Dealer/Landov 23; © Monika Graff, UPI/Landov 53; © Alison Barnes Martin, Masterfile 41; © Adriano Bacchella, Nature Picture Library 49; © Biosphoto/Peter Arnold, Inc. 29; © WILDLIFE/Peter Arnold, Inc. 27; © Shutterstock 3, 4, 5, 19, 31, 33, 35, 37, 41, 43, 51, 61.

Illustrations: WORLD BOOK illustration by Roberta Polfus 13.

World Book's Animals of the World

Shih Tzu
and Other Toy Dogs

WORLD
BOOK

a Scott Fetzer company
Chicago
www.worldbookonline.com

Contents

What Is a Toy Dog?

Toy dog is the term the American Kennel Club (AKC) and other dog organizations give to certain very small dogs. Not all small dogs are toy dogs, but all toy dogs are small. The smallest breed in the toy-dog group is the chihuahua *(chee WAH wah)*, which ideally stands about 5 inches (13 centimeters) tall at the shoulder and weighs from 1 to 6 pounds (0.5 to 2.7 kilograms).

Some toy dogs are smaller versions of breeds of larger dogs. For example, the toy poodle is a toy version of the standard poodle. Other toy dogs, such as the Shih Tzu *(shee dzoo)* and chihuahua, are found only as toy-sized dogs.

Dogs are not always placed in the same group everywhere. The Shih Tzu is considered to be a toy dog in the United States. In Canada and Australia, it is grouped with the nonsporting dogs. In the United Kingdom, the Shih Tzu is considered to be a utility dog.

A playful Shih Tzu

7

How Did Breeds of Toy Dogs Develop?

A breed is a group of dogs that have the same type of ancestors. Because breeds of dogs were developed many centuries ago, we do not know exactly how they were developed. The first toy dogs were probably smaller versions of regular-sized dogs of a breed. People probably bred two unusually small dogs of a particular breed and, by repeating that process, over time much smaller dogs of a breed were the result.

Because toy dogs were not working dogs—that is, they did not hunt or serve as watchdogs, for example—having such a dog was seen as a sign that the owner was rich. In the past, a person would have to be rich to be able to afford to keep a dog just for fun.

A standard poodle
and toy poodle

9

When and Where Did the Shih Tzu Breed First Appear?

The Shih Tzu is one of the oldest dog breeds in the world. *Shih Tzu* means "lion" in Chinese. Shih Tzu is used as both the singular (one Shih Tzu) and plural (two or more Shih Tzu) form of the noun.

Shih Tzu were valued in China because they looked something like the lions drawn by traditional Chinese artists. Some experts think that modern Shih Tzu are descended from dogs that Buddhist monks from Tibet gave to the royal family in China in the 1600's. Tibet is in western China.

Shih Tzu have been very popular in China for centuries. Members of the royal families that ruled China kept Shih Tzu as pets. As with other toy dogs, keeping a Shih Tzu was seen as a sign of wealth.

Shih Tzu in New York City, 1969

What Does a Shih Tzu Look Like?

The Shih Tzu is a small dog—ideally, between 8 and 11 inches (20 to 28 centimeters) tall at the shoulder. Most Shih Tzu weigh between 9 and 16 pounds (4 and 7 kilograms).

The Shih Tzu has a round, broad head and large, round eyes. The muzzle (mouth, nose, and jaw) of a Shih Tzu is very short compared with that of other dogs. That makes the Shih Tzu's face look a little flat.

Shih Tzu have a long, silky coat. This fur can grow so long as to sweep along the ground if it is left untrimmed. Shih Tzu fur can come in many different color combinations, including red and white, black and white, and brown and white.

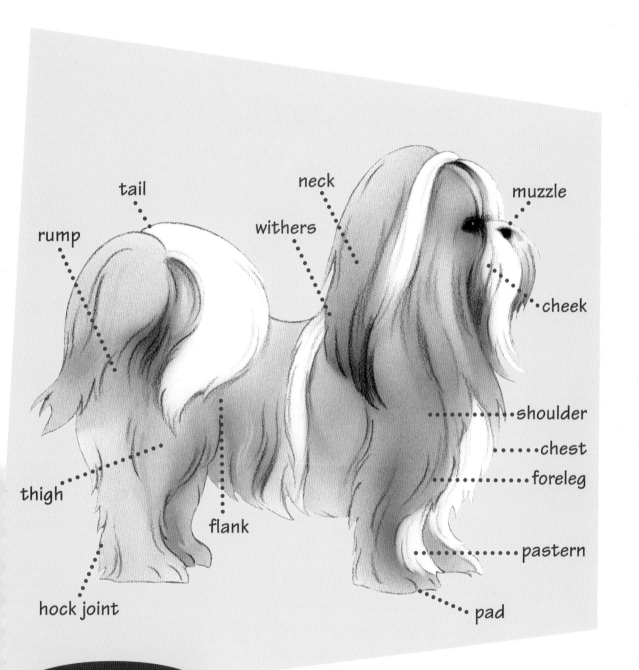

tail

neck

muzzle

withers

rump

cheek

shoulder

chest

foreleg

thigh

flank

pastern

hock joint

pad

Diagram of a Shih Tzu

What Kind of Personality Might a Shih Tzu Have?

Shih Tzu were bred to be companion dogs, so they generally have sweet personalities. They are friendly and fun-loving. These dogs make wonderful lap dogs—that is, they like to sit on a person's lap. They are also playful and enjoy toys. Shih Tzu are even known to present their owners with toys as "gifts" when they return home.

Many people think of toy dogs as being yappy—prone to barking with a loud, shrill bark. Most Shih Tzu are quiet, though they may bark when left alone, or to let you know that they want something, such as a treat.

Shih Tzu like company, and they may become stressed if left alone for long periods. They can also be stubborn, so it is important to properly train your dog to respect your commands.

A happy Shih Tzu on a beach

Is a Shih Tzu
the Dog for You?

Shih Tzu are friendly, loving dogs that would be a good choice for many people who want a dog. Their small size makes them especially good for people living in apartments or small houses.

Because Shih Tzu shed less than many other breeds of dog, they can sometimes be a good choice for people with allergies *(AL uhr jeez)*. Every person is different, however, and before you buy a Shih Tzu, you should try to be around one to see how you react if you have dog allergies.

Shih Tzu do not need a lot of exercise, so they can make good companions for people who are elderly or disabled. They may not be the right choice for people who want to take long walks or be outside most of the time. They tend to be very gentle and are good dogs for families with small children.

A Shih Tzu and its owner

What Should You Look for When Choosing a Shih Tzu Puppy?

A puppy is a big responsibility. If your family decides to get a puppy, you might begin to research different breeds by talking to a veterinarian or other dog owners. The Internet also has much information on dog breeds.

Once your family has decided that the Shih Tzu is the right dog breed, you will need to find a good breeder. A club that specializes in your breed will often be able to provide the names of breeders in your area. (See page 64 for a list of Web sites, including sites for Shih Tzu clubs.) Dog shows are another place where you might go to find dog breeders.

Before deciding on a puppy, your whole family should visit the breeder. Like people, puppies react differently to different people. Look for a dog that gets along with all members of your family.

18

Shih Tzu puppies

Should You Get an Older Shih Tzu Instead of a Puppy?

All puppies, even puppies of smaller dog breeds, are a lot of work. If your family is very busy with school, work, and activities, you may not have time to take care of a puppy. You will need to let your puppy outside to relieve itself at each mealtime and playtime. An active three-month-old Shih Tzu needs to be fed four times during the day and have about as many play sessions. In other words, it needs to be let outside about eight times a day, or about every two hours.

Getting an older dog can have many benefits. When you get a puppy, you are not sure what the dog's personality will be. When you get an older dog, you know it will keep the same personality. Because older dogs are usually already trained, they are less work. Sometimes, however, they may also have bad habits that are difficult to break.

Older Shih Tzu need lots of sleep.

Should You Consider
a Rescue Shih Tzu?

A rescue dog is a dog that has been abandoned or lost by its owners. Many local and national organizations of specific dog breeds take in, or rescue, dogs belonging to their breed. These dogs then need to find new homes.

Rescue dogs can be a good choice for many families. They are less expensive than dogs bought from a breeder. Plus, you are taking a dog that really needs your help. However, there may be health or personality problems with a rescue dog that cannot be discovered just by looking at the dog. Before choosing a rescue dog, you should try to get as much information as possible about the dog's past and health.

The Internet has many groups that are involved in Shih Tzu rescue. A Web site that is set up especially for rescuing Shih Tzu in the United States is Shih Tzu Rescue <http://www.usshihtzurescure.com>.

A rescue Shih Tzu
and its owner

What Does a Shih Tzu Eat?

All dogs need a healthful diet with different nutrients, or nourishing things. Dogs, however, need different nutrients than people do. That's why dogs do better when they are fed dog food rather than table scraps (human food).

Because toy dogs are so small, they do not need a lot of food. This means that it is especially important to make sure the food they do eat is nutritious. Your veterinarian can advise you about the best kinds of prepared dry or wet dog food to give your Shih Tzu. The specific food your dog eats will depend on how old and how active it is. Water is also very important to a dog's health. Be sure that fresh water is always available for your pet.

Some experts think dogs should never eat human foods, while others feel that occasional treats are okay. Certain human foods, however, can harm or even kill a dog, including chocolate, grapes, soft drinks, raisins, and sugarless candies. Do not feed your pet anything unless you know it is safe.

24

A Shih Tzu eating

Where Should a Shih Tzu Sleep?

Dogs, especially puppies, need a lot of sleep. A dog bed or small crate with a towel on the bottom gives your Shih Tzu a place to rest and sleep. You can also put cushions and small toys in the crate. You should make sure that any soft bedding or towels used in the crate are washable. This will help protect your dog from fleas.

If you buy a dog crate that is approved for airline travel, you can use the same crate when traveling by plane or car.

Many people enjoy having a dog sleep on their bed with them. Shih Tzu are small enough to do this, but once your dog gets into this habit, it will be very difficult to get it to stop.

Dog beds give Shih Tzu
a safe place to rest
and sleep.

How Do You Groom a Shih Tzu?

A Shih Tzu has two long coats of fur: a soft undercoat and a coarser outer coat. Because of this long, double coat, Shih Tzu need a lot of grooming. Some owners have their Shih Tzu's fur trimmed short. This can reduce the amount of grooming needed.

Shih Tzu should be brushed and combed once a day to prevent painful mats (clumps of tangled fur) from forming. A Shih Tzu's face also needs to be cleaned once a day. Many people put the hair around the face into a topknot to keep it out of the Shih Tzu's eyes.

A Shih Tzu's nails need to be cut every other week. This can be a tricky job, so you should ask an adult to help you.

Because dirty fur mats more easily than clean fur, Shih Tzu need to be bathed regularly. Your dog may need to be bathed every two to three weeks. Always brush your dog before and after shampooing.

Shih Tzu require more grooming than short-coated breeds of dogs.

What About Training a Shih Tzu?

Training a Shih Tzu will help it to learn how to behave and how to communicate. Training makes for a much happier dog and owner. Because they are small and friendly dogs, Shih Tzu are generally easy to train. But it is important that dog owners get advice, or even take classes, on how to properly train a dog.

It is best to start researching how to train your dog before it comes home. You may also want to talk to people who own an older Shih Tzu and get advice on what sorts of problems may occur.

Consider taking your puppy to dog obedience school as soon as it is old enough—at about six months. This leaves little time for the dog to pick up bad habits. Do not worry if your dog is older, however. Older dogs can be trained. And, older dogs also benefit from obedience school.

Training any dog takes time and patience.

31

What Kinds of Exercise or Play Are Needed?

Like all dogs, Shih Tzu love to go for walks. Because of their small size, however, a quick walk around the block three times a day is generally enough exercise. If you have a fenced yard, you can let your Shih Tzu run around outside by itself for short periods. This will allow it to get enough exercise, even if you cannot go for a walk.

Shih Tzu like to be at home, and because their long hair attracts sticks and bugs, they are not really suited for long walks, especially in wooded areas.

At home, if you provide your Shih Tzu with a variety of chew toys and cuddly toys, it should be able to entertain itself. However, your Shih Tzu's favorite activity will still be spending time with you.

Shih Tzu love to play with toys.

Should You Breed Your Shih Tzu?

Most people should not breed their dogs, however fun it sounds to have cute puppies around. There are many more pets in the world than people who want to take them in. It is estimated that up to 8 million dogs and cats go into shelters in the United States every year, and only about half of them find homes. One out of four dogs in shelters is a purebred.

The most helpful thing you can do is to have your vet perform an operation—called spay or neuter—on your dog that prevents it from being able to have puppies. (A vet spays female dogs and neuters male dogs.) This way, you do not make the problem of unwanted animals worse.

If you get a rescue dog, you may be asked to have the dog spayed or neutered. A good breeder may ask you to do the same.

Newborn Shih Tzu

35

Are There Special Organizations for Shih Tzu Owners?

In the United States, the main organization for people who love Shih Tzu is the American Shih Tzu Club. There are also more than 15 local clubs throughout the country. Similar organizations outside the United States include the Canadian Shih Tzu Club and the Shih Tzu Club (the United Kingdom's club).

The main goal of these clubs is to provide reliable information about Shih Tzu. They can put breeders and dog owners in touch with each other and help people understand how best to take care of their dogs. Local clubs may also sponsor gatherings and events for Shih Tzu and their owners. Dog organizations can be a good place to get recommendations on everything from dog training to breeders to veterinarians.

You can find out more about these organizations by visiting the Web sites listed on page 64.

A curious Shih Tzu

How Do Shih Tzu Help People?

There are many groups of dogs that have been bred or trained to help people. Some dogs make excellent seeing eye dogs, or do other tasks for people with disabilities.

Some Shih Tzu have a special job that allows them to help people. These dogs have been trained as therapy dogs. A therapy dog acts as a companion to sick or elderly people. These dogs might visit people in a hospital or nursing home. Shih Tzu, with their loving personalities, make wonderful therapy dogs.

Shih Tzu are loving companions.

What Are Some Other Toy Dog Breeds?

The American Kennel Club (AKC) sets the standards (accepted rules) for dog breeds in the United States and keeps track of pedigrees. It divides dog breeds into groups. The AKC places the Shih Tzu into the toy dog group. Other breeds that are considered to be toy dogs by the AKC include the affenpinscher *(AH fuhn PIHN shuhr)*, the Brussels griffon (*GRIHF uhn)*, the chihuahua *(chee WAH wah)*, the Chinese crested, the pug, and the toy poodle.

Groups similar to the AKC exist in Australia, Canada, and the United Kingdom. These organizations group breeds differently. The Canadian Kennel Club (CKC), the Australian National Kennel Council (ANKC), and the Kennel Club (KC) in the United Kingdom group toy dogs similarly, though they group the Shih Tzu differently. (See page 6.)

A Japanese chin

A Yorkshire terrier

A Pomeranian

A papillon

What Is a Chihuahua?

A chihuahua is the smallest type of toy dog. Chihuahuas stand about 5 inches (13 centimeters) tall at the shoulder and weigh from 1 to 6 pounds (0.5 to 2.7 kilograms). To be in a dog show, a chihuahua must weigh less than 6 pounds (about 3 kilograms).

Chihuahuas are named for a state in Mexico, the country where many experts believe they were first bred. The most popular type of chihuahua has a smooth coat, which features very short fur. Chihuahuas also come in a long-coated variety.

Although recent television commercials and movies have made chihuahuas very popular, they are not a good choice for families with very small children. The chihuahua's size makes it a little fragile for rough handling.

A chihuahua

What Is a Poodle?

A poodle is a breed of curly-coated dog. A poodle's coat can come in a variety of colors, including apricot, black, brown, and cream. Poodles come in three sizes: standard, miniature, and toy. The toy poodle is 10 inches (25 centimeters) or under at the shoulder; the miniature poodle is between 10 and 15 inches (25 and 38 centimeters); and the standard poodle is over 15 inches.

Experts believe that standard poodles were originally bred in Germany as water retrievers *(rih TREE vuhrz)*. Poodle owners used to shave much of the dog's hair to help it to better move through the water. Owners left patches of the hair long over the dog's joints and chest, however, to help keep those areas warm. (See page 9 for an example of a poodle with this haircut.)

A toy poodle

45

What Is a Pug?

Like Shih Tzu, pugs are a very old breed of dog. Most experts believe that pugs are from Asia. The record of their earliest appearance in China dates to about 100 B.C.

Portuguese and other European traders brought pugs to Europe in the 1500's. The Dutch royal family began keeping pugs in the 1600's, and this helped to make them a popular dog in Europe for many years.

Pugs are one of the largest dogs of the toy group. They are known for their comical, flat face. Their flat noses can sometimes cause serious breathing problems.

Pugs are an especially good breed of toy dog for households with small children.

A pug

47

What Is an Affenpinscher?

An affenpinscher is a small dog that looks a bit shaggy. It has a wiry coat and bushy eyebrows that hang down over its eyes. Tufts of hair stick out all over its face, and it has a mustache.

The name *affenpinscher* comes from the German words meaning monkey terrier. The Germans thought the affenpinscher's face to be monkeylike. In France, the affenpinscher is called the *Diablotin Moustachu* (*DEE ahb luh tuh MOO stah shoo*), which means "moustached little devil."

Ideally, an affenpinscher weighs about 8 pounds (3.6 kilograms) and stands only about 10 inches (25 centimeters) high at the shoulder. Its coat can be many colors, but black is common.

The affenpinscher was bred to hunt rats in farmhouses and stables. It is still known as a small but strong dog. This dog is alert and playful and makes a loyal pet.

An affenpinscher

What Is a Chinese Crested?

A Chinese crested is a breed of small dog. It stands from 11 to 13 inches (28 to 33 centimeters) high at the shoulder and weighs from 5 to 10 pounds (2.3 to 4.5 kilograms).

There are two kinds of Chinese cresteds: hairless and powderpuff. The hairless Chinese crested has soft, flowing hair only on the head (called the crest), the tail (called the plume), and the lower legs and feet (called the socks). Hairless skin covers the rest of the body. The skin can be any color or a combination of colors. Because the hairless Chinese crested has no fur to protect the skin from sunburn, owners sometimes use sunscreen on this dog. The powderpuff Chinese crested has a soft, fluffy coat of hair over the entire body. Both varieties can be born in the same litter.

Hundreds of years ago, Chinese merchants carried the dogs on sailing vessels and thus introduced them to other countries throughout the world. The Chinese crested probably came originally from Africa.

A hairless Chinese crested

51

What Is a Dog Show Like?

Dog shows have become very popular in recent years. They are a way for dog owners to find out how well their animal conforms (matches up to) the standards (accepted rules) for its breed. In addition to being judged on looks, some dogs also compete in trials that judge how well they have been trained.

Dog shows are run by such organizations as the American Kennel Club (AKC) in the United States. The Canadian Kennel Club (CKC), the Kennel Club (KC) in the United Kingdom, and the Australian National Kennel Council (ANKC) also sponsor shows in their home countries. Groups dedicated to individual breeds, such as the American Shih Tzu Club, also sponsor shows for their breed. All of these groups have certain rules about how a dog must appear and behave. Many groups allow young people to participate in junior divisions at their shows.

Not all purebred dogs are show quality. Whether or not a dog is considered show quality has nothing to do with how good a dog it is, or what kind of pet it will make.

Preparing Shih Tzu for a dog show

Are There Dangers to Dogs Around the Home?

In some ways, dogs, especially puppies, are like small children. They tend to want to chew and bite new and unfamiliar items. Puppies have to be trained not to chew things like electrical cords and shoes.

Dogs should only chew specially made dog toys. These toys are designed for a dog's strong teeth. If a dog chews on a baby toy, the toy may break into small pieces. This could choke the dog.

Cleaning supplies and poisons meant to get rid of mice or bugs can quickly poison a small dog. Keep these items out of your dog's reach.

Also, small dogs can easily jump through small openings in windows, so be sure to put screens on all of your windows.

Because of their flat noses, Shih Tzu can drown in large or deep bowls of water. Make sure the only bowl of water standing around is its own shallow drinking bowl.

A Shih Tzu at home

What Are Some Common Signs of Illness?

Toy dogs tend to live long, healthy lives. Most live about 12 to 15 years. But every breed of dog has its own set of health problems. Because there are so many different types of toy dog, there is no one set of illnesses associated with toy dogs.

Shih Tzu tend to be very healthy. Their long fur helps them to stay warm in cold weather. However, this fur can make the dog too hot in warm weather. The Shih Tzu's flat nose may make this worse by making it harder for the dog to breathe. Because of this, a Shih Tzu can become overheated quickly. On hot summer days, avoid going on long walks, and be sure to give your dog plenty of water.

The most common signs of illness in any dog are a change of behavior and loss of appetite. Because dogs cannot tell us how they feel, it is important that you closely watch your dog and report any strange behavior to a veterinarian.

Get to know your dog's normal behavior so you can tell when it feels sick.

What Routine Veterinary Care Is Needed?

Like people, dogs need regular medical checkups to stay healthy. Finding a good veterinarian is an essential first step to becoming a dog owner.

When you take your dog to the veterinarian, he or she will perform a physical exam, checking the dog for possible problems. Your dog will also need regular vaccinations *(VAK suh NAY shuhnz)*, or shots. These shots help to protect your dog from getting certain illnesses. Some dog illnesses, like rabies, can be dangerous to people. Depending on where you live, the law may require you to make sure your dog has had vaccinations, and to keep a record of the shots.

Your veterinarian can also give you advice on feeding and grooming your dog.

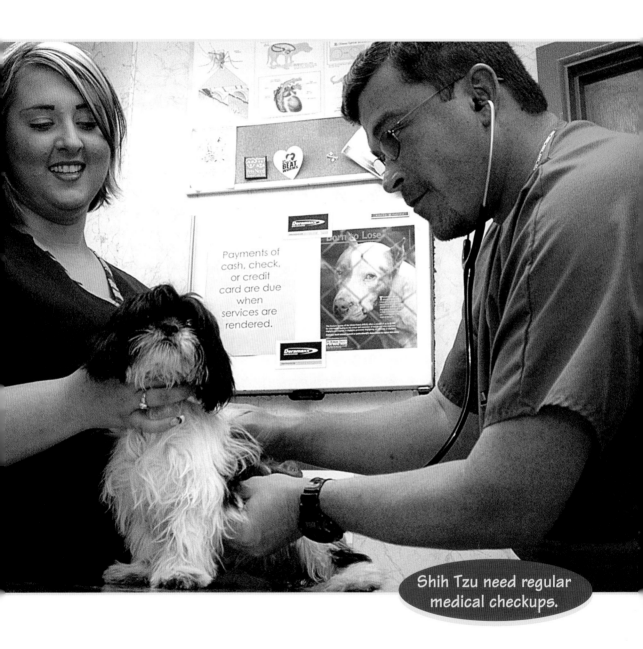

Payments of cash, check, or credit card are due when services are rendered.

Shih Tzu need regular medical checkups.

What Are Your Responsibilities as an Owner?

A responsibility is a job or task that you promise to do. You may already have certain responsibilities, such as taking care of a younger sibling, getting good grades, or keeping your room clean.

Owning a dog gives you more responsibilities. If you choose to get a dog, you must honor those responsibilities, even if you are sick, tired, or just bored. Some of the responsibilities of owning a dog include feeding, grooming, and caring for it. You also have a responsibility to clean up after your dog, and to make sure it does not harm or bother other people.

Owning a dog is a big responsibility, but the friendship you and your dog share will also bring you much joy.

Shih Tzu can bring families great joy.

Toy Dog Fun Facts

→ Shih Tzu were first brought to the United States by American soldiers returning from the United Kingdom after World War II (1939-1945). They quickly became a popular breed and were recognized by the American Kennel Club in 1969.

→ In the early 1500's, a pug named Pompey is said to have saved the life of his royal Dutch owner, William II, Prince of Orange. Pompey heard Spanish troops approaching and barked and licked his owner's face until Prince William woke up. The prince was able to run to safety. After this, the pug became the official dog of the House of Orange.

→ In the 1800's, Josephine, the wife of the French Emperor Napoleon, owned a pug. When Napoleon was in prison, the couple used the dog to send messages back and forth to each other.

Glossary

allergy A reaction, or change, caused by something that would not ordinarily be harmful to humans, such as animal fur or dust.

ancestor An animal from which another animal is directly descended. Usually, *ancestor* is used to refer to an animal more removed than a parent or grandparent.

breed To produce animals by carefully selecting and mating them for certain traits. Also, a group of animals having the same type of ancestors.

breeder A person who breeds animals.

groom To take care of an animal, for example, by combing, brushing, or trimming its coat.

litter The young animals produced by an animal at one birthing.

neuter To operate on a male animal to make it unable to produce young.

pedigree A record of an animal's ancestors.

purebred An animal whose parents are known to have both belonged to one breed.

rabies A disease caused by a virus that destroys part of the brain and almost always causes death. Rabies is transmitted by the bite of an animal that has the disease.

retriever A hunting dog trained to retrieve (find and bring back) game.

shed To throw off or lose hair, skin, fur, or other body covering.

spay To operate on a female animal to make it unable to have young.

topknot Fur pulled up into a tuft on top of the head, similar to a ponytail.

Index (**Boldface** indicates a photo, map, or illustration.)

For more information about Shih Tzu and other toy dogs, try these resources:

Books:
The Complete Dog Book for Kids by the American Kennel Club (Howell Book House, 1996)
Shih Tzu by Lynn M. Stone (Rourke, 2009)
Shih Tzu by Jaíme Sucher (Barron's Educational Series, 2000)
Superpuppy: How to Choose, Raise, and Train the Best Possible Dog for You by Jill and Daniel Manus Pinkwater (Clarion Books, 2002)

Web sites:
American Kennel Club
http://www.akc.org
American Shih Tzu Club
http://www.americanshihtzuclub.org/

Australian National Kennel Council
http://www.ankc.org.au
The Canadian Kennel Club
http://www.ckc.ca/en/
The Canadian Shih Tzu Club
http://www.canadianshihtzuclub.ca/
Humane Society of the United States
http://www.hsus.org
The Kennel Club
http://www.thekennelclub.org.uk/
Shih Tzu Club (United Kingdom's club)
http://www.theshihtzuclub.co.uk/index.php

Dog Classification

Scientists classify animals by placing them into groups. The animal kingdom is a group that contains all the world's animals. Phylum, class, order, and family are smaller groups. Each phylum contains many classes. A class contains orders, an order contains families, and a family contains genuses. One or more species belong to each genus. Each species has its own scientific name. Here is how the animals in this book fit into this system.

Animals with backbones and their relatives (Phylum Chordata)
Mammals (Class Mammalia)
Carnivores (Order Carnivora)

Dogs and their relatives (Family Canidae)

Domestic dog .... *Canis familiaris*